D1872131

DAFFODIL SCISSORS

by Philip Ridley

SAMUEL FRENCH

samuelfrench.co.uk

ISBN 978-0-573-12040-4

www.samuelfrench.co.uk

www.samuelfrench.com

For Amateur Production Enquiries

United Kingdom and World
excluding North America
plays@SamuelFrench-London.co.uk
020 7255 4302/01

Each title is subject to availability from Samuel French, depending upon country of performance.

ABOUT THE AUTHOR

Philip was born in the East End of London. He studied painting at St Martin's School of Art. He has written many highly regarded and hugely influential plays: the seminal *The Pitchfork Disney*, the multi-award-winning *The Fastest Clock in the Universe*, *Ghost from a Perfect Place*, *Vincent River*, *Mercury Fur*, *Leaves of Glass*, *Piranha Heights*, *Tender Napalm* (nominated for the London Fringe Best Play Award), *Shivered* (nominated Off-West End Best New Play Award), *Dark Vanilla Jungle* (winner of an Edinburgh Festival Fringe First Award), *Radiant Vermin*, *Karagula* and *Tonight With Donny Stixx*, plus several plays for young people: *Karamazoo*, *Fairytaleheart*, *Moonfleece* (named as one of the 50 Best Works About Cultural Diversity by the National Centre for Children's Books), *Sparkleshark*, *Brokenville* and *Feathers in the Snow* (shortlisted for the Brian Way Best Play Award).

He has also written novels for children, including *Scribbleboy* and *Mighty Fizz Chilla* (both nominated for the Carnegie Medal) and the bestseller *Krindlekrax* (winner of both the Smarties Prize and WH Smith's Mind-Boggling Books Award), the stage play of which – adapted by Philip himself – was premiered at the Birmingham Rep Theatre in 2002.

In 2010 Philip, along with song-writing collaborator Nick Bicât, formed the music group *Dreamskin Cradle* and their first album, *Songs from Grimm*, is available on iTunes, Amazon and all major download sites. Philip is also a performance artist in his own right, and his highly-charged readings of his ongoing poetry sequence *Lovesongs for Extinct Creatures* (first embarked on when he was a student) have proved increasingly popular in recent years.

In 2012 *What's On Stage* named him a Jubilee Playwright (one of the most influential British writers to have emerged in the past six decades). Philip has won both the Evening Standard's Most Promising Newcomer to British Film and Most Promising Playwright Awards. The only person ever to receive both prizes.

Other plays by PHILIP RIDLEY
published and licensed by Samuel French

ADULT

The Pitchfork Disney

The Fastest Clock in the Universe

Ghost from a Perfect Place

Vincent River

Mercury Fur

Leaves of Glass

Piranha Heights

Tender Napalm

Shivered

Dark Vanilla Jungle

Radiant Vermin

Tonight with Donny Stixx

Karagula

FOR YOUNG PEOPLE

The Storyteller Sequence

Karamazoo

Fairytaleheart

Sparkleshark

Moonfleece

Brokenville

FOR FAMILIES AND CHILDREN

Krindlekrax

Feathers in the Snow

INTERVIEW WITH THE AUTHOR

You wrote Daffodil Scissors for the Royal National Theatre, didn't you?

I did, yes. It was part of their Connections scheme.

Plays written for young people?

That's right. I'd already written several other plays for Connections: *Sparkleshark, Moonfleece, Brokenville* and *Karamazoo*. But *Daffodil Scissors* was a little different in that it was part of a new strand. It was called Assembly Connections: plays written to be done by a whole class at a school's morning assembly.

So...how did the play come together?

Not the dreaded "where did you get the idea from?" question?!

Afraid so.

Well... a lot of the initial thoughts were triggered by the brief itself. The play was to be performed by a class, so the cast size needed to reflect that. It was also important for me that no child in the class should feel excluded: so there are big parts with lots of words for pupils that want those, and smaller parts with less words for pupils who feel more comfortable with that. It's also possible to be on stage – as part of a crowd - and say nothing! Also, for those pupils who wanted to be part of the show but didn't relish being up on stage at all, there are other aspects they can be involved with, like design and costume and so on. In short, I wanted *Daffodil Scissors* to be a play in which, hopefully, everyone could be part of it in some way.

The biggest "design" activity, I suppose, is the hats?

Yes, yes! I think that could be great fun. Every member of the class can design and make a hat that reflects who they are. I've seen some wonderful productions where the play ends with a sort of catwalk fashion show: every pupil proudly displaying their headgear. Some of the creations I've seen – in both schools and drama groups – have been quite breathtaking, believe me!

And with the initial brief of doing the play at a school assembly... that dictated the running time, I suppose?

Yes. It's quite short. And it should be performed at great pace. All scenes go straight into the next. I've seen some productions go at such a lick they took my breath away. But that's part of the thrill of it, I think.

And what can you say about the actual "story" aspects of the play?

Again, the initial brief contributed here. It was intended to be done in schools, so it made sense to set it in a school. And, consequently, it made sense to explore those things every child going to school (including me!) experiences: how to fit in, making friends, peer pressure, bullying.

You didn't have to wear extraordinary hats, did you?

No, no. Not that I would have minded! But I did wear rather eye-catching bow-ties. My mum chose them for me. Like a lot of people in the East End of London at that time, she worked in tailoring. She had an acute sense of fashion. I was always "well turned out", as the saying goes. I look at school photos from that time and there's all my classmates in jeans and T-shirts...and there's me in button up shirt and bow-tie. Don't get me wrong, I loved the bow-ties. But they did make me – how shall I say? – "stand out" somewhat. I remember the ties were on elastic, so classmates were always pulling them so they'd snap back on my nose or forehead. But I never mentioned any of this to my mum. Not just because – like Daffodil in the play – I didn't want to upset a parent, but because, as I say, I enjoyed wearing them. I liked the way they made me look different. But at school – as in life – we're constantly weighing up the balance between individuality and conformity. Do I sacrifice eccentricity for the sake of popularity? Or will my eccentricities, in time, become the *reason* I'm popular.

Which is what happens to Daffodil.

Yes.

Did it happen to you?

I'm still waiting.

Friendship is freedom.
Anonymous

CHARACTERS

DAFFODIL
DAD
TELLY
BASH
FIRST BULLY
SECOND BULLY
THIRD BULLY
FOURTH BULLY
FIFTH BULLY
SIXTH BULLY
SEVENTH BULLY
STAR
ACTION
KA-POW
TEACHER
FOOTBALLER
COMMENTATOR JACK
COMMENTATOR BOB
GOALIE
FOOTBALL FAN
SECOND FOOTBALL FAN
BAG LADY
PEST CONTROL
COCKROACH EXTERMINATOR

DAFFODIL Hello, everyone.

My name is Daffodil Scissors.

I haven't got

any friends.

Not *one!*

This is why...

DAD Morning, Daffodil.

DAFFODIL Morning, Dad –

Now, watch this! –

...Dad, can I go out to play

after school today please?

DAD "Go out to play"?!

You mean not come

home straight away?!

Oh, why would you

want to do that?

Oh, why? Why?

DAD *starts to cry.*

DAFFODIL Dad always cries

if I say I want to go out to play.

DAD Oh, I do, I do.

DAFFODIL He cries if I say

I want to make friends.

DAD *cries louder.*

Tell me why

you're crying, Dad?

DAD I'm crying because
...oh, what would I do
if I *lost* you.
Lost *you* like
I lost your poor
departed *Mum?*

DAFFODIL But you *won't*
lose me, Dad.

DAD But I might.
Only home is safe.
If you go out to play
and make friends...
anything could happen.

DAD *bursts into tears again.*

DAFFODIL Okay, okay.
I *won't* go out to play.
I won't make friends.
I'll come straight home
where everything is safe
...and *nothing* happens.

DAD You promise?

DAFFODIL I promise.

DAD *calms down.*

DAD Oh, I feel a lot better now.
By the way, I've made you a new hat!

DAFFODIL Dad's hats!
Wait to you get
an eyeful of this!

DAD *produces new hat.*

It is quite extraordinary.

DAFFODIL See what I mean?

DAD Put it on, Daffodil!

DAFFODIL *puts the hat on.*

Like it?

DAFFODIL Love it! Time I left for school!

DAD Don't take your hat off.

DAFFODIL I won't.

DAD Cross your heart?

DAFFODIL Cross my heart.

DAFFODIL *goes to school –*

BASH Here comes Daffodil.

FIRST BULLY What're you wearing on your head today, Daffodil?

SECOND BULLY Is it a mutant pineapple on your head, Daffodil?

THIRD BULLY Has someone's been sick on your head, Daffodil?

BASH AND BULLIES *(chanting)* Daffodil, Daffodil – Stupid Hat! Who could ever be friends with *that*?

BULLIES *laugh and move away.*

DAFFODIL *(calling after* **BULLIES***)* I'd rather look like *me* than *you*. I've got...individuality!

STAR *steps forward.*

STAR I agree.

DAFFODIL Who're you?

STAR They call me "Star".

DAFFODIL Why?

STAR It's what I'm going to be.

DAFFODIL A *pop* star? A *film* star?

STAR Oh, I don't care.

DAFFODIL I haven't seen you before.

STAR It's my first day at this school.

DAFFODIL Where'd you go before?

STAR Another school. Miles away.

DAFFODIL How *many* miles?

STAR Two hundred and twenty-six.

DAFFODIL Where d'you live now?

STAR The street opposite the supermarket.

DAFFODIL I know where that is!

STAR Why don't you visit me after school?
We can go out to play and be friends.

DAFFODIL What's your door number?

STAR Twelve.

DAD *(calling)* Daf – fod – dil!

DAFFODIL I'm at school, Dad!

DAD It's over now! You should be home!

DAFFODIL Oh! Okay.
(at **STAR***)* Sorry, Star.
I have to go home.

DAFFODIL *goes to* **DAD**.

DAD I'm making you a new hat.

DAFFODIL Another one?

DAD It may be my most ambitious yet.

DAFFODIL Shall I make you a sandwich, Dad?

DAD That'd be scrumptious.

DAFFODIL There's hardly anything in the fridge
except cheese...or cheese.

DAD Er... I'll have a cheese sandwich please.

DAFFODIL You need to go to the shops
to get other things
to put in sandwiches.

DAD I'm too busy making hats to go to the shops.

DAFFODIL Here's your cheese sandwich.

DAD Thank you.

DAFFODIL Dad...
can I go out to play?

DAD "Go out to play"!?
After what you promised
this morning!?

DAFFODIL But I met someone
called Star and –

DAD "Star"!?
And what am I supposed to do
while you're out playing with
this Star?

DAFFODIL You can watch the telly.

DAD *Alone?*

Starts to cry.

But... Daffodil!

We always watch the television *together!*

Oh, how can you break your promise to me?

How can you break your promise to me?

How can you break –?

DAFFODIL Okay, okay!
I'll turn the telly on!
We'll watch it together.

DAD What a good idea!

DAFFODIL *turns the television on.*

TELLY Hello. This is the news… Bad, bad, bad, bad, bad etc.

DAD Oh, the news is nothing but bad lately.

DAFFODIL I'll change the channel.

Switches channels.

TELLY And now for our film: "Everything Is Nice As Nice Can Be."

DAD Oh, this sounds nice.

TELLY People are nice,
houses are nice,
weather is nice,
dogs are nice…

DAD Turn it up, Daffodil.

DAFFODIL *turns volume up.*

TELLY POLITICIANS ARE NICE,
TRAFFIC WARDENS ARE NICE,
LAWYERS ARE NICE –

STAR Where'd you get to yesterday?

DAFFODIL Eh?

STAR It's next morning. We're in the school playground.

DAFFODIL Oh. Okay.

DAFFODIL *goes to* **STAR.**

STAR I thought we were going to play out
and be friends.

DAFFODIL I had to watch telly with my dad.

ACTION *has arrived.*

ACTION Not that "Nice" film. It was *so* boring!

DAFFODIL Who're you?

ACTION Action.

STAR It's a nickname.

DAFFODIL *(at* **ACTION***)* How'd you get it?

STAR Action wants to be a film director.

ACTION Lights! Camera! Action!

DAFFODIL I've never seen you in this school before.

ACTION I joined today.

STAR Action was bullied at his last school.

DAFFODIL *I'm* bullied at *this* one.

ACTION Then we'll have to stick together won't we?

DAFFODIL, STAR and **ACTION** We *will*!

BULLIES Daffodil, Daffodil – Stupid Hat!
Who could ever be friends with – ?

STAR Leave Daffodil alone, you bullies!

ACTION Daffodil's hats are wonderful.

STAR They give him individuality.

ACTION We *like* individuality.

STAR And we *like* Daffodil.

ACTION and **STAR** Daffodil is our friend!

BASH *has now arrived.*

BASH Who could *ever* want
Daffodil as a friend?!

STAR and **ACTION** Who's this?

DAFFODIL Bash.

BASH Nickname.

ACTION How'd you get it?

BASH I like to bash things! – BASH!

BULLIES BASH!

DAFFODIL Bash is the *leader* of the bullies.

BASH We're Bash and the Bullies.

BASH and **BULLIES** BASH AND THE BULLIES – BASH!

FOURTH BULLY Listen, you two.
You can't be friends with Daffodil *and*
be friends with us.

FIFTH BULLY No you can't!

BASH So choose.
Daffodil...or *us*?

STAR AND ACTION ...Daffodil!

BASH *and the* **BULLIES** *gasp in shock.*

DAD *(calling)* Daf – fod – dil!

DAFFODIL I'm at school, Dad.

DAD It's *after* school now. Come home!

DAFFODIL Oh. Okay.

STAR Don't stay at home watching telly
all with your dad again, Daffodil.

ACTION No. Come out to play with us.

DAFFODIL I'll try.

STAR and **ACTION** Promise?

DAFFODIL Promise.

DAFFODIL *goes to* **DAD**.

DAD Turn the television on, Daffodil.

DAFFODIL Er... Dad –

DAD You're not going to ask
if you can go out to play

and make friends again, are you!?
Because if you *do* I think I might
cry and *cry* and *cry*
and – this time! –
never stop.

DAFFODIL Er...no!
Of course I wasn't going to ask that.
I was going to ask...
what channel shall I put on?

DAD *You* decide.

DAFFODIL *turns television on.*

TELLY The same, the same, the same, the same, the same...

DAD What's this?

DAFFODIL Pop songs.

DAD Oh, they all sound the same lately. Change channels.

DAFFODIL *switches channels.*

TELLY Now for our film: "Life Is Cosy And Ever So Sweet."

DAD Oh, this sounds cosy and sweet.

TELLY People are cosy and ever so sweet,
houses are cosy and ever so sweet,
dogs are cosy and ever so sweet.

DAD Turn it up, Daffodil.

DAFFODIL *turns volume up.*

TELLY KITTENS ARE COSY AND EVER SO SWEET,
FLUFFY TEADY BEARS ARE COSY AND –

STAR Good morning, Daffodil.

DAFFODIL It's next day now?

STAR It is.

ACTION We're in the school playground.

DAFFODIL I see.

Good morning, Star.

Good morning, Action.

ACTION Good morning, Daffodil.

STAR Daffodil,

you didn't come round yesterday

so we could all go out to play.

ACTION We had lots of fun – Didn't we, Star?

STAR We did, Action.

DAFFODIL I wanted to play out but –

STAR Don't tell us.

You had to stay at home –

ACTION And watch telly with your dad all night again.

DAFFODIL That's right.

KA-POW Not that "Cosy and Sweet" film. It was *so* boring!

DAFFODIL Who're you?

ACTION and **STAR** This is our new friend.

KA-POW Ka-Pow!

DAFFODIL A nickname?

KA-POW Ka-Pow!

STAR Ka-Pow wants to be an actor.

ACTION An action hero!

KA-POW Ka-Pow! Ka-Pow! Ka-Pow!

DAFFODIL Are you going to this school now too?

KA-POW Ka-Pow!

TEACHER *blows whistle.*

TEACHER Everyone, it's the local schools' football final today.

DAFFODIL I *hate* football.

KA-POW Ka-Pow!

ACTION Ka-Pow obviously *loves* football.

KA-POW Ka-Pow! Ka-Pow!

TEACHER The final is between our team.

TEAM *cheers.*

And the team from the school down the road.

TEAM *boos and hisses.*

As you know, our school has *never* won the final.
So give them all your support and cheer a lot and –

FOOTBALLER Sir!

TEACHER What's wrong?

FOOTBALLER I've got a belly-ache.

TEACHER But you're our number one striker!

FOOTBALLER I can't help it.
That fish burger I had for breakfast
has gone right through me.

TEACHER But if you don't play –

FOOTBALLER I *can't!*

Rushes off, clutching stomach.

TEACHER Oh, what're we going to do?

KA-POW Ka-Pow!

TEACHER Can you play?

KA-POW Ka-Pow!

TEACHER Let the match begin!

COMMENTATOR JACK It's the last ten minutes of the match, Bob.

COMMENTATOR BOB Time is rushing by, Jack.

COMMENTATOR JACK No one's scored yet.

COMMENTATOR BOB It's going to be a draw.

COMMENTATOR JACK Any players stand out?

COMMENTATOR BOB This new player – Ka-Pow. What flare!

COMMENTATOR JACK Ka-Pow's got the ball now!

COMMENTATOR BOB Ka-Pow's rushing for the goal.

GOALIE Stay away from my goal!

COMMENTATOR JACK Ka-Pow's getting past everyone!

COMMENTATOR BOB What a player!

COMMENTATOR JACK Ka-Pow's kicked the ball!

ALL Goal!

FOOTBALL FAN I'm starting the Ka-Pow Fan Club!

SECOND FOOTBALL FAN I'm joining!

TEACHER *blows whistle.*

DAFFODIL We've won!

KA-POW *lifts trophy.*

ALL There's only one Ka-Pow!
Ka-Pow's our striking wow!
We're the champions now!
All power to Ka-Pow!

DAFFODIL You're the most popular
person in the whole school, Ka-Pow!

KA-POW Ka-Pow!

DAFFODIL Everyone wants to be
your friend, Ka-Pow.

KA-POW Ka-Pow!

DAFFODIL How does it feel, Ka-Pow?

KA-POW Ka-Pow!

DAFFODIL I'm *never* going to be popular.
and have lots of friends.
Not while I wear these hats.

ACTION There's nothing wrong with your hats.

KA-POW Ka-Pow! Ka-Pow! Ka-Pow!

STAR I agree Ka-Pow. They *do* give him individuality.

DAD *(calling)* Daf – fod – dil.

STAR Make sure you come round to my house later.
We're all going out to play.

ACTION We are.

KA-POW Ka-Pow!

STAR And we *really* want you
to play with us.

ACTION We do.

KA-POW Ka-Pow!

STAR So find a way of getting
away from your dad.

DAFFODIL I'll try.

DAD *(calling)* Daf – fod – dil.

DAFFODIL *goes to* **DAD.**

Turn thc television on, Daffodil.

DAFFODIL *turns the television on.*

TELLY Tonight's film is called
"Life Is Sugary Sweetness Full of Sugary Softness."

DAFFODIL Er... Dad –

DAD You're not going to ask
to go out to play again, are you?
Because if you do –

DAFFODIL No!
Don't cry!
Of *course* I'm not
asking to go out to play.
I was going to say...
I best go to the shops
to get some shopping.

DAD "Shops"?!
"Shoppng"!?

DAFFODIL We need something more
in the fridge than cheese
...and cheese.

DAD But the film's just beginning!

DAFFODIL I'll buy some chocolate
while I'm at the shops.
We can eat sugary sweetness
while we watch "Sugary Softness".

DAD What a good idea!
Here's some money.
Don't be long.

DAFFODIL I won't.

DAFFODIL *goes to* **STAR, ACTION** *and* **KA-POW**.

STAR and **ACTION** and **KA-POW** Hello, Daffodil!

STAR You've come out to play!

DAFFODIL I told Dad I was going to the shops.

STAR You *lied* to him!?

DAFFODIL I'll go to the shops
on the way back
so it won't be a *total* lie.

ACTION and **STAR** Perfect!

KA-POW Ka-Pow!

BASH Hello, Daffodil.

DAFFODIL What *you* doing here?

BASH I'm friends with Ka-Pow now – Right, Ka-Pow?

KA-POW Ka-Pow!

BASH Ka-Pow!

ACTION Bash wants to be an action hero too.

STAR And Bash has got something to say to you.

DAFFODIL To *me?*

STAR Yes. *(At* **BASH***)* Tell Daffodil, Bash.

BASH I'm... I'm sorry I picked on you.
It was stupid and nasty of me.
I can see that now.
I only did it because –

STAR There's no excuses for bullying, Bash!

ACTION Not ever!

KA-POW Ka-Pow!

DAFFODIL You did it because I wore these stupid hats.

STAR Will you please *not* refer to your hats as stupid.

ACTION They are *not* stupid.

KA-POW Ka-Pow! Ka-Pow!

STAR They are distinctive.

ACTION They are...what's another word?

BASH Different.

ACTION Exactly.

DAFFODIL Oh, I know, I know.
But it seems like the thing
that gives me individuality

and distinctiveness
and makes me different
is also the thing that
gets me picked on and bullied.
Perhaps I should stop wearing them and –

STAR No!
You should *never* stop
wearing your hats
just to fit in!

BASH Yes, he should.
If that's what he *wants*.

STAR No. He shouldn't.

BASH He should.

STAR He shouldn't.

BASH He should.

DAFFODIL There's no point
in arguing about it.
I *couldn't* stop wearing them
even if I wanted to.

BASH Why?

DAFFODIL My dad takes such
care making them.

BASH So?

DAFFODIL It would upset him
if I stopped wearing them.

BASH So?

DAFFODIL I'm scared of upsetting him.

BASH You shouldn't be such a coward.

STAR Oh, I *do* wish you'd stop having opinions, Bash.

You're muddling everything up.

DAFFODIL Answer me this, Bash!

Who's the biggest coward?

Me for being bullied because

I don't want to upset my dad.

Or *you* for bullying me because

you're bigger and stronger than me.

ACTION Wow! What a speech!

KA-POW Ka-Pow!

BASH I didn't really understand a word of it.

DAFFODIL It's a bit contrived, I agree.

ACTION I disagree.

...Well, okay, it might be a *bit* contrived.

But it still sounded great

You should write something!

DAFFODIL "*Write* something"?!

ACTION A film!

STAR *I'll* act in it.

ACTION *I'll* direct it.

KA-POW Ka-Pow! Ka-Pow!

BASH *I'll* kick and jump *with* you!

KA-POW and **BASH** Ka-Pow!

STAR Oh, come on, Daffodil! *Write* it!

We can all have such fun!

DAFFODIL I'd *love* to. Really. But –

DAD *(calling)* Daf – fod – dil!

DAFFODIL I can't ignore that!

Walks away.

Oh, I'm never going to be able

to play out and have friends
and write a screenplay
that's made into a blockbuster film
that goes on to win lots of Oscars
and makes me world famous
and rich beyond my wildest dreams.

BAG LADY Why the long face?

DAFFODIL Who are you?

BAG LADY Call me Bag Lady.

DAD *(calling)* Daf – fod – dil!

BAG LADY Is that your dad calling?

DAFFODIL He wants me to go home.

BAG LADY He always wants you home I bet, eh?

DAFFODIL How'd you know?

BAG LADY I'm very wise.

DAD *(calling)* Daf – fod – dil!

DAFFODIL I'm never going to be able
to play out and have friends
and write a screenplay
that's made into –

BAG LADY We've heard all that!
Take this!

Hands **DAFFODIL** *a plastic bag.*

DAFFODIL What is it?

BAG LADY A hamburger.

DAFFODIL *peeks inside plastic bag.*

DAFFODIL Ugh! It stinks!

BAG LADY It's five days old.

DAFFODIL I can't eat *this*.

BAG LADY You're not *supposed* to eat it.

DAFFODIL Then what *am* I supposed to with it?

BAG LADY Put it under under your bed.

DAFFODIL But why should I put –?

BAG LADY D'you want to stop your dad
calling out for you all the time
and crying if you want to play out
and make friends or not?

DAFFODIL Of *course* I do!

BAG LADY Then do as you're told!

DAFFODIL So is this hamburger...magic?

BAG LADY It might be.

DAFFODIL And are you a...*witch?*

BAG LADY Please don't put a label on me!

Walks off.

DAD Where have you been, Daffodil?
I've been calling and calling!

DAFFODIL Sorry, Dad.

DAD I was so worried.
It's made me feel quite ill.
I'm going to bed.
Goodnight.

DAFFODIL Goodnight.

Puts hamburger under his bed.

There!
The hamburger's under my bed.

DAD Good morning, Daffodil.

DAFFODIL Good morning, Dad.

DAD I've finished making your new hat.

What d'you think?

DAFFODIL It's very…big.

DAD I told you.

My most ambitious yet.

Put it on.

DAFFODIL *puts it on.*

Like it?

DAFFODIL Of course I do.

Goes to school.

FIFTH BULLY Here comes Daffodil.

SIXTH BULLY What you wearing on your head *today*, Daffodil?

SEVENTH BULLY Is that a dead mongoose on your head!?

FOURTH BULLY Is it solidified elephant earwax on your head?

BASH I *like* your new hat, Daffodil.

BULLIES *gasp!*

May I try your new hat on please, Daffodil!

BULLIES *gasp louder.*

DAFFODIL *gives* **BASH** *his hat.*

FIRST BULLY Don't do it, Bash!

FIFTH BULLY You'll regret for the rest of your life, Bash!

BASH *puts hat on.*

BULLIES *gasp louder still.*

SEVENTH BULLY *faints.*

BASH How's it look?

STAR Very stylish.

KA-POW Ka-Pow!

ACTION Film star glamorous!

BASH I LOVE THIS HAT!

FIRST BULLY *I* want a hat like that!

SECOND BULLY *I* want a hat like that too!

FOURTH BULLY And me!

BULLIES Yeah! Yeah!

FIRST BULLY Daffodil...can your dad come to school and make hats for *all* of us?

DAFFODIL I... I don't know. You see...

FIRST BULLY What?

DAFFODIL Well, Dad never goes out.

THIRD BULLY What? *Never* never?

DAFFODIL Well...*hardly* ever.

STAR You do have a tendency to exaggerate sometimes.

DAFFODIL I confess I do.

ACTION That's the writer in him.

THIRD BULLY Why does your dad hardly ever go out?

DAFFODIL It's all because of my mum.

STAR I didn't think you had a mum.

DAFFODIL I haven't now.
But I did when I was a baby.

KA-POW Ka-Pow? Ka-Pow? Ka-Pow?

DAFFODIL I can't remember much about her at all, Ka-Pow. All I *do* remember are her tattoos.

BASH I *love* tattoos.

ACTION So do I.

FIRST BULLY How many tattoos did your mum have?

DAFFODIL Two.

SECOND BULLY Where?

DAFFODIL One on each arm.

THIRD BULLY What was on the left arm?

DAFFODIL A daffodil.

SEVENTH BULLY What was on the right arm?

DAFFODIL Scissors.

ACTION Her baby's name on her arms!
What a concept!

STAR Your mum sounds a wonderful woman.

DAFFODIL She was.
Dad loved her from the moment
they first met at art school.

STAR What sort of art
did your mum study?

DAFFODIL Fashion.
She wanted to be cobbler.

BASH There's no need for bad language.

DAFFODIL Cobbler's not bad language.

STAR It means Daffodil's mum
was studying how to make shoes.
Correct, Daffodil?

DAFFODIL Correct, Star.

STAR And your dad – I assume –
was studying to be a milliner?
Correct, Daffodil?

DAFFODIL Correct, Star.

BASH What's a...milliner?

DAFFODIL Someone who makes hats.
Dad and Mum had plans to open a shop.
"From Your Head To Your Toes".

SIXTH BULLY So what happened to you mum, Daffodil?

DAFFODIL Mum went to climb a mountain.

FIRST BULLY Why?

DAFFODIL Because it was there.

ACTION Where was "there"?

DAFFODIL Miles away.

STAR How *many* miles?

DAFFODIL About one hundred and three.

BASH So...what happened?

DAFFODIL Mum climbed to the top of the mountain.
And then...she disappeared.

ACTION "Disappeared"?

BASH You mean she...fell off?

DAFFODIL Yes.

STAR Oh, I'm so sorry, Daffodil.

DAFFODIL And since then...
Dad has been afraid to go outside.

STAR And he keeps you as close as possible
because he's afraid you might
fall off a mountain too.

BASH But there's no mountain's round here.

DAFFODIL There's mountains to fall off *everywhere*, Bash.
And most of them are not even mountains.

ACTION Listen to that! What a way with words!

BASH I didn't understand it personally.

DAFFODIL It was a bit wilfully obscure, I admit.

ACTION Nonsense!
It was poetic perfection!

STAR Oh, Daffodil!
Please write something for us all to act in.

ACTION And for me to direct.

DAFFODIL But I could *never* write a whole film script.
It's far too difficult to do.

STAR Write a stage play then.

ACTION Yeah, writing a stage play is easy.

BASH *Anyone* can write a stage play.

STAR Lots of movie stars get spotted in stage plays.

SECOND BULLY *I* want to be in a stage play!

THIRD BULLY *Me* too.

BULLIES And *me*! And *me*!

BASH We can all wear your dad's
individual and
distinctive and
different hats –
Right, bullies?

BULLIES Right, Bash!

DAD *screams.*

DAFFODIL Dad!

Rushes to **DAD.**

What is it?

DAD Your bedroom!

Stands on chair.

DAFFODIL What?

DAD Look!

DAFFODIL *looks.*

DAFFODIL Cockroaches!

DAD Hundreds!

DAFFODIL Thousands!

DAD Oh, I don't want
to see the them!

Covers his eyes.

Phone for help, Daffodil!

DAFFODIL *dials number on phone.*

PEST CONTROL Hello, Pest Control here?

DAFFODIL We've got cockroaches, Pest Control.

PEST CONTROL We'll send someone over right away.

DAD Oh, *how* did we get cockroaches?
I do the housework every day!

DAFFODIL I can't tell him it's because
of the rotting, stinky hamburger under my bed.
But how are cockroaches
attracted by a rotting, stinky hamburger
going to help me be able to
play out and make friends and –?

COCKROACH EXTERMINATOR Hello!

DAFFODIL Are you the Cockroach Exterminator?

COCKROACH EXTERMINATOR I am.
Where are the cockroaches coming from?

DAFFODIL Under my bed.

COCKROACH EXTERMINATOR Hang on!
Your shoes need re-heeling.

DAFFODIL Wh-what?

COCKROACH EXTERMINATOR Oh! Sorry.

I've been doing that a lot lately.

DAFFODIL Noticing other people's shoes?

COCKROACH EXTERMINATOR Yes.

DAFFODIL Why?

COCKROACH EXTERMINATOR I think I may have been a cobbler before I...

DAFFODIL Before you *what*?

COCKROACH EXTERMINATOR Oh, it doesn't matter.

DAFFODIL No. Tell me, tell me.

COCKROACH EXTERMINATOR Before I fell off a mountain.

DAFFODIL You fell off a mountain! *When?*

COCKROACH EXTERMINATOR Years ago!

I fell off and I woke up in hospital.

But I had lost my memory.

And all my identification.

So I had no idea who I was

or where I came from.

DAFFODIL So what did you do?

COCKROACH EXTERMINATOR I roamed everywhere.

DAFFODIL Hoping you'd see something

to triggers your memory?

COCKROACH EXTERMINATOR That's right.

DAFFODIL And does anything *here*

trigger your memory?

COCKROACH EXTERMINATOR Well...to be honest...

this place *does* feel

somewhat familiar.

DAFFODIL Tell me...have you got any tattoos?

COCKROACH EXTERMINATOR One on each arm!

Daffodil on this arm.

And –

DAFFODIL Scissors on the other arm.

COCKROACH EXTERMINATOR How did you know?

DAFFODIL Dad! Dad!

Come here!

DAD I don't want to see the cockroaches.

DAFFODIL Just look at the Cockroach Exterminator!

Slowly, **DAD** *removes hands from his eyes.*

He looks at **COCKROACH EXTERMINATOR.**

COCKROACH EXTERMINATOR *gives* **DAD** *a double take.*

Then looks longer.

Pause.

Then –.

COCKROACH EXTERMINATOR Gary!

DAD *(at* **COCKROACH EXTERMINATOR***)* Tracy!

DAFFODIL *(at* **COCKROACH EXTERMINATOR***)* Mum!

COCKROACH EXTERMINATOR Daffodil!

DAFFODIL Dad!

DAD Daffodil!

COCKROACH EXTERMINATOR Tracy!

DAD Gary!

DAFFODIL All right, all right, enough!

COCKROACH EXTERMINATOR My memory!

It's all coming back!

Oh, it's *so* good to be home!

DAD With you by my side
I can open the door wide.

COCKROACH EXTERMINATOR With you by my side
I won't ever fall off a mountain again.

DAFFODIL Dad? Can I go out to play and –?

DAD Yes, yes, clear off.
I'm busy with your mum.

DAFFODIL *(at* **STAR** *and the others)* And so that's why
I can now come out and play with you all!
Any time I like!

ACTION What a story!

STAR Amazing!

BASH Breathtaking!

KA-POW Ka-Pow!

FIRST BULLY You should write it down.

DAFFODIL I have.

ACTION You mean...?

DAFFODIL It's the stage play we're going to do!

KA-POW Ka-Pow!

STAR What part will I play?

DAFFODIL We can all play ourselves.

ACTION The boy's a genius!

DAFFODIL And others from school can play the other parts.

DAD I'll be your Dad.

COCKROACH EXTERMINATOR I'll be your Mum.

TEACHER I'll be the Teacher.

BAG LADY I'll be the Bag lady.

COMMENTATOR JACK I'll be the Sports Commentator.

COMMENTATOR BOB I wanted to be that.

DAFFODIL We'll have *two* Commentators.

FOOTBALL FAN And a Football Fan?

SECOND FOOTBALL FAN Me as well!

DAFFODIL I'll work it in, yes.

OPERATOR You need somcone to answer the phone at Pest Control.

DAFFODIL The part's yours.

FIRST BULLY What about the rest of us?

DAFFODIL You're the Bullies.

SECOND BULLY But we're *not* bullies anymore.

THIRD BULLY How will we *ever* find our motivation?

ACTION I'll direct you!

BASH And will your dad make us hats?

DAFFODIL I'm afraid he's far too busy
having a good time with my mum.

BASH Then we'll just have to make our *own* hats.

FIRST BULLY It'll be like a project.

STAR A hat that expresses who we are!

ACTION Our individuality!

BASH Our different...ness.

KA-BOOM Ka-Pow!

SECOND BULLY My hat'll be made out of dinosaur teeth and chewing gum.

THIRD BULLY Mine'll be dead mice and spit.

KA-POW Ka-Pow! Ka-Pow! Kap-kap-kap! Ka-Pow! Ka-Kap! Pow! Pow! Ka-Pow! Pow-Kap! Kap-Kap! Pow! Pow!...Pow.

BASH And we'll wear our hats with pride.

KA-POW We will!

They all stare at **KA-POW**.

Then–

ACTION Any idea how the stage play will begin, Daffodil?

DAFFODIL With me!

I'll stand in the middle of the stage.

And I'll say, "Hello, everyone.

My name is Daffodil Scissors!"

Property List

New hat. It's quite extraordinary (p2)
Plastic bag (p18)
Hamburger (p19)
New hat (p20)
Chair (p24)
Phone (p25)

Sound/Effects

Daffodil turns the television on (p6)
Switches channels (p6)
Daffodil turns volume up (p6)
Daffodil turns the television on (p9)
Switches channels (p9)
Daffodil turns volume up (p9)
Teacher blows whistle (p10)
Teacher blows whistle (p12)
Daffodil turns the television on (p13)

Lightning Source UK Ltd.
Milton Keynes UK
UKHW020954110422
401398UK00006B/470

9 780573 120404